What Have I Got
Myself Into?

What Have I Got Myself Into?

Mark Ritchie
&
Andy Flannagan

New Wine Press

New Wine Press
an imprint of RoperPenberthy Publishing Ltd
23 Oatlands Drive
Weybridge
Surrey
KT13 9LZ

Scripture quotations are from The Holy Bible, New International Version
Copyright © 1978 by New York International Bible Society. Published by
Hodder & Stoughton.

ISBN 978-1-905991-65-5

Typeset by **documen**, www.documen.co.uk
Cover design by KentKreations
Printed in the United Kingdom

Mark, with his wife Tamzin, their son Jordan and daughter Keziah are based in Nottingham, England. Mark has told his stories all over the world and loves to make people laugh and think. His attitude that God desperately wants to connect with us comes through in whatever stage he finds himself on. Mark is also a passionate Nottingham Forest fan, which is a little unusual for a Scotsman!

Andy Flannagan is married to the very gorgeous Jenny, treasures some great friends, and is the new Director of the Christian Socialist Movement based from Westminster. Andy is passionate about politics and the Church, encouraging Christians to see engagement with politics as mission. Andy also continues to perform, speak, lead worship and play a lot of cricket. His proudest moment, as an Irishman, was captaining England's Barmy Army during the last Ashes series. His new worship songs and resources are available for free from www.andyflan.com.

Helen was not a Christian when she heard Mark Ritchie speak. But she felt compelled by the message of the cross and she went on this amazing journey called Christianity.

CONTENTS

Introducing...

Andy: *"It had seemed like a good idea at the time, what with the pamphlet dropping through the door and the weather outside looking so welcoming. A marathon would certainly look impressive on the CV, and may even impress a few of the other runners in the park. What harm could signing up do? Well, quite a lot. Putting aside the potential obstacles and hardships that the marathon itself would throw up, there was the fear of failing to finish and of letting all the sponsors down. The blisters and the tight muscles, the cramps and the oh so smelly socks, were just window dressing for the main event: getting through the wall that all runners talk about. It is much easier to think of reasons to abandon the resolution you so recently made, than to find that courage to take the first step. Where on earth to start from?*

A couple of men were out hunting in the woods when one of them suddenly falls to the ground. He doesn't seem to be breathing, and his eyes are rolled back in his head.

The other guy whips out his mobile phone and dials 999. In a panic, he gasps to the operator: "Please help me! I think my friend might be dead! What can I do?"

The operator, in a calm, soothing voice, says: "Just take it easy. I can help. First, let's make sure he's actually dead."

There is a silence and then a shot rings out. The guy's voice comes back on the line. "Okay. Done that. Now what?"

You may well be able to identify with that sense of panic. All this God stuff may be starting to make sense, but your totally understandable fear is, "What's going to happen next? Am I likely to have to purchase sandals or start eating lentils? Will I look like a hypocrite? Do I have to learn to sing in harmony?" You may be thinking, "What have I done?" but hopefully you're not about to grab a shotgun. So the question is, "Now what?"

This book is designed to help you chill out and not become an annoying, over-stressed, legalistic panicker. God made us and knows exactly what we're capable of, and the chances are the immediate expectations we put on ourselves are much crazier than his.

In the story, the guy is so keyed up that he simply follows the letter of the law, rather than employing his own brain and trusting the authority of the guy on the other end of the phone.

He was also thinking, "What am I going to do now?", and in his panicked state, his mind slavishly followed the words, but came to the wrong conclusion. The Bible talks about this life being a race, but it's not a sprint, where all is won or lost in the first 10 seconds. There's no need to panic. It's actually more like a marathon, but we'll get back to that later, because as we've just said, we've got plenty of time. This journey is about developing a relationship of trust with the One who both designed the journey and accompanies us on it.

Mark: During a marathon, there are drink stations where you take on water and get energised for the next phase of the race. It's the same with running the race of faith. This book will describe what these drink stations might look like in the context of being a follower of Jesus. We need fuel for the journey from outside of ourselves.

Our motivation to take on the water and energy we need to finish the race reaches a new level when we're not just running it for ourselves. Anyone who has run a marathon for a charity testifies to the extra motivation they gain at those moments of total pain or despair, from the fact that what they are doing is making someone else's life better. This is why so many of the folks who last longest serving in their communities are Christians. They have a reason to stay involved and a God who gives them the power to stay involved. So this is not just another self-help manual with a Jesus theme. If all you're looking to do is sort your own life out, you may as well not cross the starting line. Following Jesus means running a race where other people's needs loom larger in our vision than our own needs do.

We should point out at this stage that nothing you are about to read comes from our personal marathon experience. We can categorically state that we have never, nor do we intend to participate in any race longer than 100m, never mind a marathon. All we have gleaned is from friends who have impressively made it through the 26 miles and 385 yards that constitutes the marathon. The more you experience life, the more you realise that it is a long, winding road with many ups and downs. Hopefully your journey won't end up like Pheidippides, the guy who allegedly ran the first marathon, who collapsed and died having delivered the vital message that he had been carrying from the battle in Marathon to Athens.

Some of the things that we'll talk about may feel like disciplines, but they aren't for the sake of appearing pious or holy. Like the training that a marathon runner needs to do, they are simply the daily exercises that allow us to run well. They allow us to enjoy the race, rather than getting injured, running out of breath or pulling up with cramp. I've seen too many folks pull out of the race even though everything looked good on the outside. It's the equivalent of the keen new runner who buys the reflective Lycra gear, the expensive Nike trainers, and the wristwatch that measures your pulse, yet doesn't actually get out and do any training. So are you ready to start?

DRINK STATION ONE:

Where Are We?

Andy: *Having sobered up, your friends remind you of what you did last night: sign up for the cross country marathon in Big Story country. Heaving at the thought of all that mud, you set your mind to at least looking at the course to gauge whether you ought to just give up now. Eventually you find yourself at the start line, exhausted just by the hill from the bus stop. The marathon has many hills, screes and rivers to ford. There are long sections through green pastures and the dog walkers you encounter speak warmly of the views from the peaks, but warn of tough times if the weather turns.*

Unable to say exactly why and seemingly against your better judgement, you find yourself wanting to take on this marathon course. It seems more worthwhile an endeavour than anything else you have noticed before. But first, some preparation is needed. What are the entry requirements and how much does it cost?

It is easy to pay lip service to those to whom we should be more grateful and it is all too easy to name check accomplished people in order to be bathed in their reflective glories. Jesus, however, asks for just one thing of us: that we follow him. (John 21:19b) Name checking Jesus may make us feel better, but won't necessarily make us a follower, nor will just paying lip service to his accomplishments on earth and in heaven. Jesus isn't some insecure demagogue who needs more scalps on his scoreboard to prove he's the best god. He doesn't need to get into "My dad's bigger than your dad" type arguments. He desires us to follow him because he made us and knows what is best for us, and he longs to have an intimate relationship with us. He wants us to follow him throughout the whole course of our life that he has set before us. How does that work?

You don't see too many marathon runners with rucksacks on their back, so we may want to identify and throw off any baggage that may hinder us in this race.

Mark: When I was in Africa I went on Safari. The driver was going out to get wood for the fire, and he asked for volunteers. I volunteered as it sounded like fun. I thought we'd just be collecting some wood and throwing it in the back of the truck. It was a big four-by-four straight out of Jurassic Park, so as we were driving through the bush, I asked him to show me how fast the truck could go. He got some serious speed on it and it was great fun but then when it came to finding the wood, he stopped by this huge dead tree lying in the bush, and chained the tree to the back of truck. Needless to say, the truck could hardly get up any speed for obvious reasons. The thing that we were chained to was holding us back. The return journey was a lot less fun. So for you, what might be chained to the back of your jeep? Is it guilt, or fear, or a bad habit, or an unhealthy relationship that is holding you back from being everything you can be? Yes, we were still moving, but the truck was not able to perform in the way that it was designed to.

This is not just a clever illustration that I have invented, it is simply a reflection of the truth found in the Bible and expressed most clearly in Hebrews 12:1b, 'Let us throw off everything that hinders and the sin that so easily entangles, and let us run with perseverance the race marked out for us.'

Have you ever seen the movie, The Mission? It stars Jeremy Irons, Robert De Niro and Liam Neeson. There is a scene where Robert De Niro, who has just killed his brother in a duel, is travelling to train to become a priest amongst an Amazonian tribe that until recently he was hunting. He is desperate for forgiveness of his actions and so carries along, on this journey through the forest, all his belongings from his previous life as a soldier; armour, weapons, shields and ammunition. He climbs waterfalls and rock faces carrying this burden and eventually he reaches the top still weighed down by this burden, but then he slips and falters and the weight threatens to drag him back down. But one of the Amazonian tribe reaches down with a knife and cuts the rope that links him to his burden. He cries with forgiveness and belief; the tribe he used to hunt could have chosen to use that knife to kill him, but instead they choose to save him and thus they found peace together.

Fix your eyes ahead. If you're continually looking around to check on the great hunk of wood, or burden from your past that you're dragging behind you, you can't fix your eyes dead ahead. You don't enjoy the view. And you may hit an obstacle or pothole that you didn't see coming. How do we fix our eyes ahead?

Andy: Before you dive into the detail, it is probably more important to get an overview of the "Big Story" of the Bible, to see where Jesus fits in and begin to answer those questions of, 'how do I qualify', and, 'how much does it cost?' Here follows a useful summary.

Perhaps the best way to understand what God asks of us is to begin with looking at how he relates to the world. What does he want for the world? How has he engaged with us over the course of history?

We know that, in the beginning, God created the heavens and the earth. In a cosmic act of creativity beyond our comprehension, God made something beautiful from nothing. He created a magnificent world which was itself creative; full of harmony and full of possibilities.

And he made human beings in his own image and likeness (Genesis 1:27), to carry something of his authority and presence into the world. God blessed humanity and gave us the job of nurturing and stewarding his creation; we were meant to ensure that this amazing creation became all that it could be, as it continued to expand and reach its potential. We do this by walking with God, following his lead.

However, as we know, humanity resisted God's command, preferring instead to do its own thing, to be its own god.

And what followed, if we read Genesis chapters 3-11, was generations of strife, violence, pain and disaster. God's vision of life on earth, of creativity and harmony and everyone having enough, was twisted and broken into a horrific nightmare. Humanity fell from God's grace – surely enough to make him abandon us, abandon the whole project.

But God did not give up on us or his creation. He sought to redeem the earth, restoring it to what was intended. He started speaking to an obscure old farmer in what is now Iraq, and made a deal with him. God said to this farmer:

'I will make you into a great nation,
And I will bless you;
I will make your name great,
And you will be a blessing.
I will bless those who bless you,
And whoever curses you I will curse;
And all peoples on earth
Will be blessed through you".'

(Genesis 12:2-3)

God's covenant or agreement with Abraham promised him that his descendants would be a special people who would exist to be a blessing to 'all peoples on earth'. The blessing they received was never intended to stop with them or to simply serve their own ends – the mission was always for everyone else. Abraham's descendants would be a force for good in the world, a light to the nations, a demonstration of what it meant to know God and to live life as it was meant to be lived. A just people, living in relationship with God and others.

The Exodus and the Law

Abraham's descendants did grow into a nation. They found themselves being forced into slavery in Egypt, being oppressed, and they cried out to God. He heard their cries and rescued them from this injustice, rescued them from Egypt. And it was then that God spoke to them about what it meant to be his people and about the mission and the life he was calling them to. The foundation of their identity as God's people was rooted in their experience of being rescued from a life of injustice, oppression and poverty.

It was in this time in the wilderness that God gave them his law, sharing his heart and his priorities with them. In Exodus 19 he tells them he is calling them to be a kingdom of priests. In ancient near-eastern religion, priests were the go-betweens, representing God to the people and the people to God, and their costumes usually carried a visual representation of the nature of the god in question. So when God calls this whole nation of ex-slaves to be a kingdom of priests, he's telling them that their life as a community will be a visual representation in the world of his character and his priorities, and moreover, as he promised Abraham, they will carry God's blessing to the rest of humanity. So, how they live as a people really matters.

And so he gives them many laws to structure their life together. He wants them to be a just people, living in healthy relationship together and caring especially for the weak and vulnerable in their midst – the widows and orphans among them. He teaches them fair economic principles, where resources are shared fairly and laws such as the Jubilee mean that debts are cancelled every seven years and the land is restored to its original owners every 50 years, helping prevent inequality.

God wants to ensure that no-one in their community goes without food or becomes crippled by debt. He teaches them that the foundation of their community life is love and reverence for him, and a commitment to loving their neighbour as themselves. And God tells them that it is his intention that other nations would hear and see how they live and say, 'Surely this great nation is a wise and understanding people.'

The prophets

But, of course, the people rebelled again and again, rejecting God's way. The laws were forgotten, the poor were oppressed by the rich and the people followed gods created in their images. The religious ceremonies became empty rituals which meant nothing; their leaders failed to maintain justice or defend the needy.

So God sent prophets like Isaiah, Jeremiah, Amos and Micah, to remind them of his ways of justice and wholeness, and to condemn their religion which was full of sacrifices and rituals but had turned away from the heart of God's purposes. The prophets' two main concerns were directed at the heart of the law: idolatry – not loving God with their whole heart, failing to understand that their whole identity and mission were wrapped up in their relationship with Yahweh; and injustice – not loving their neighbour as they loved themselves but allowing injustice, oppression and selfishness to grow up in their midst. Isaiah said:

'Stop bringing meaningless offerings, your incense is detestable to me…I cannot bear your evil assemblies… even if you offer many prayers I will not listen. Your hands are full of blood, wash and make yourselves clean… stop doing wrong, learn to do right, seek justice, encourage the oppressed, defend the cause of the fatherless, plead the case of the widow.'

(Isaiah 1:11-17)

God wanted his people to be a light to the other nations, a blessing to all peoples but to do this they had to return to what God had asked of them. The prophet Micah (6:8) once summed up what God required of them in these well-known words: 'To act justly, to love mercy and to walk humbly with your God.'

But among this story of frustration and failure, of fresh chances lost and justice ignored, God also spoke about someone who would come and lead the way in bringing restoration and renewal to God's creation.

God was going to intervene and send somebody who would declare God's rule over the earth and lead his people back to their true identity and mission; someone who would fulfil other words of Isaiah:

The Spirit of the Sovereign Lord is on me,
because the Lord has anointed me
to preach good news to the poor.
He has sent me to bind up the broken hearted,

to proclaim freedom for the captives
and release from darkness for the prisoners

                                        (Isaiah 61:1)

Jesus

And so, as the New Testament begins, Jesus is introduced as the son of David, the son of Abraham. Jesus stands in continuity with everything that God has been doing up to this point, fulfilling and embodying God's mission to restore and redeem the earth.

And as he begins his public life, Jesus identifies himself as the figure in Isaiah 61, reading out that passage in the synagogue to define his mission from the outset. And as he goes on he talks more and more about what he calls the good news – the fact that the kingdom of God is here. God has been calling the Jewish people to embody and live out the kingdom of God – God's rule of wholeness and justice – over the preceding centuries. But now Jesus is here to embody it perfectly, to bring heaven to earth, to see God's will done on earth as it is in heaven and to invite others to be reconciled with God and to join in.

Jesus sets about making this kingdom into a reality by transforming the lives of people around him – especially those who are poor, disabled and excluded. He demonstrates that the kingdom of God restores us back into relationship with our creator and brings a life of justice, freedom, a new start, inclusion and abundance – good news to those who are poor and oppressed.

According to Jesus, the kingdom touches every part of our lives, not just some spiritual sphere. There is another way to live: the way we were always meant to live. And people no longer have to be born into the Jewish race to be part of it – now because of Jesus' sacrifice on the cross, his death and resurrection, the way has been made for all of us to be reconciled to God and experience the kingdom life. Everyone is invited in, if they turn from their own ways and follow Jesus.

Conclusion

This is the story of which we are a part. This is the story which the Holy Spirit teaches us to live. And we know that there is a glorious end to it. God has promised to unite heaven and earth and make all things new. The kingdom which we are pursuing here and now will last forever. Through us, God is building his everlasting kingdom, a place of mercy where people are loved and included, where they are forgiven and can come to know him for themselves, where justice is established, where the poor and the downtrodden and the rich and the lonely are restored and transformed. Does this big picture give you a better idea of why you might want to run the race, and who has run it before you?

DRINK STATION TWO:

Enjoying a Balanced Diet and Exercise Regime

|||||||||||||||||||||||||||||||||||||||||||||||||||||||||||||||||||||||||||||||||||||||||||||||||||||||||||||||||||||||||||||||||||||

Mark: *"It was getting easier to run early in the morning as the sun was rising just in time to return home. The shoes had been carefully chosen by how few blisters they promised to impart and the fluorescent running top made it clear to all and sundry that here was one serious and committed runner. If only anyone else was out to see it. It turned out that it was mostly people from outside of town who had decided to tackle this course. Indeed it turned out people thought it a little weird even talking about it, as though anyone considering such a venture was a bit holier than thou. Still, it felt great, as though each body part was finally beginning to be used to its full potential. Nothing seemed impossible: at least until the muscle aches began in earnest, but each day they hurt a little less. This daily devotion made previously insurmountable obstacles seem much less daunting. This was just one of the many unexpected, yet pleasant surprises."*

Taking time to decide whether a venture is possible or not is something Jesus extolled the virtues of. (Luke 14:28-33), 'Suppose one of you wants to build a tower. Will he not first sit down and estimate the cost to see if he has enough money to complete it? For if he lays the foundation and is not able to finish it, everyone who sees it will ridicule him, saying, "This fellow began to build and was not able to finish." Or suppose a king is about to go to war against another king. Will he not first sit down and consider whether he is able with ten thousand men to oppose the one coming against him with twenty thousand? If he is not able, he will send a delegation while the other is still a long way off and will ask for terms of peace. In the same way, any of you who does not give up everything he has cannot be my disciple.' So preparing well each day is essential to ensure the race can be run and run well. Where to start? Well, for the very basics of life a good diet is essential. Jesus knew this too but went further by saying that, 'Man cannot live on bread alone, but on every word that comes from the mouth of God.'(Matthew 4:4) How do we begin to enjoy that diet?

I once turned up at an event absolutely starving. It was 4pm and I hadn't eaten since breakfast. My stomach was beginning to threaten me with dog-like noises. The event was being held in a school, so I was pointed towards the school kitchen. When I got there I found that I was on my own, expected to fend for myself. There was a large tin of Heinz tomato soup sitting on a shelf. It seemed to call out to me. I remember picking it up and looking at the label, knowing that this would do me good, fill me up and warm the cockles of my heart. I held the tin in my hand, cherishing it as the answer to all my problems.

But there was a problem. There was no tin opener in the kitchen. I frantically checked every drawer and cupboard, and was beginning to wonder if someone had just planted the tin to frustrate me. What kind of kitchen doesn't have a tin opener?

So in my desperation I begin to bang the tin up and down on the work surface, and 2 minutes later I realise that it's just not happening. I slump on exhausted and defeated and more to the point still hungry. The sad end to the story is that my dinner ends up being 12 Ginger Nuts.

I was so frustrated because I knew the contents of the tin would do me good, and feed my soul, but I just didn't have the tools to get into it. This is how loads of people feel about the Bible. They know it's good, but the size and scale of such a big book scares them.

God cheers us on and speaks to us through the Bible, so it is important that we start reading our Bible regularly. As you read, ask God to speak to you. You will be amazed at what you hear.

So a great place to start is John's gospel. Number one, it's a story. It takes you on a very definite journey, in which you have a good sense of where you are in the story. You won't feel lost. Number two; it's the story of Jesus' life, with his actual words. He is there as a real human being, with the same struggles and joys as us. It is really inspiring to see his life as an example for ours.

Andy: Even though the Bible has been shown to be historically accurate, it is not simply a text book. The Bible is a living book, so as you read, ask God to speak to you through his Holy Spirit. You will be amazed at what you hear.

As we've mentioned before, we aren't meant to do this on our own, and through the centuries many Christians have grappled with the Bible and researched its context. We'd be mad (and arrogant) not to make use of all this accumulated wisdom. There are loads of great books and reading programmes that give commentary and explanation to bits of the Bible.

I hope this section is a real encouragement to you because making a decision to follow Jesus can be quite an emotional thing. It's also a very real thing, but inevitably when we process memories we can begin to doubt that decisions that have involved emotion are less reliable in some way. It's very reassuring to know that the reality of Jesus is not based merely on the say-so of someone like me, but also on a heavy weight of historical evidence that makes the research behind the Da Vinci code look comically featherweight.

It's also reassuring to know that we stand on the shoulders of people who down through the centuries have explored who Jesus was, and attempted to follow him. This is not a fad. And in the 21st century if you are joining this journey, you are part of a movement that is global and growing.

The Bible is a unique collection of books. There is nothing comparable in the rest of literature. It demands attention from everyone, but often its content is too challenging for us to accept, so we ignore the fact that it is a text that stands in its own right.

The Bible shows **unity** through 1500 years of writing. 66 books have been written by 40 different authors, from different places and backgrounds (who mostly didn't know each other), in three different languages, yet from start to finish, there is just one coherent unfolding story about mankind's salvation. Unity is an important concept when looking at historical texts.

Imagine assembling ten people from your town, from the **same** socio-economic background, and asking them all one big question about life. Even with this vaguely coherent group, you would definitely get many different answers. This puts the amazing unity of the Bible in context.

Or what about getting 20 people who have never met to write the individual chapters of a novel, for which none of them has the overall outline of the story. What is the likelihood of it being coherent? Pretty slim, I think you'll agree. Yet the Bible manages it.

You can break the evidences for the Bible down into 3 sections:

◊ unity + history with archaeology supporting

◊ the testimony of the early church

◊ countless lives changed

We have three **written** sources of evidence: **original Greek manuscripts**, the various **translations** and the **writings** of the early church fathers.

Here are two **historical tests** as applied to the New Testament

> **Time interval** – There are 5,500 manuscripts (hand-written copies) in existence. The earliest **copy** known was copied at just 50 years from its original writing, and then many more were copied before 250 years. Compare this to Caesar's story (1st copy 1000 years later), or the Iliad (2000yrs later)…which are both much respected historical texts.
>
> **No of copies** – The New Testament's 5,500 copies is the most of any ancient work…compare this to the stories of Catullus (3 copies), or Herodotus (8 copies).

These two factors are the most commonly used to access the reliability of historical texts…you can see that even from a historical point of view, the New Testament documents are way ahead of the field.

Also, there are 18,000 translated versions into several other languages… no other documents from that time had that sort of treatment. Further support is provided by 250 years worth of early church writings quoting from the text of the New Testament documents, which again is an important test.

Sir Frederic Kenyon, who was the former director and principal librarian of the British Museum and a top expert on ancient manuscripts said this: **"This interval between the dates of original composition and the earliest evidence becomes so small as to be in fact negligible, and the last**

foundation for any doubt that the scriptures have come down to us substantially as they were written has now been removed. Both the authenticity and the general integrity of the books of the New Testament may be regarded as finally established."

The first three gospels can be placed as having been written within 30 years of the events, because Acts (the sequel to Luke) was written before Paul's death in AD 64. They are also reliable as they were written by **eyewitnesses**, or by those who knew them that were still alive, so the documents had to stand up to public scrutiny.

It must, however, be remembered that we put our faith in a **person**, not a book.

No other book in history has changed lives like the Bible. This is not because it is more skilfully written than any other (even though it outshines most contemporary literature) but because it invites you into a relationship with the God who will change your life for the better. He may not make it easier, but he will make it better. He can't help himself.

Few books stand outside time and outside the world's self-generated ethics. I know no other book that continually challenges us and calls us to a higher standard, while all the while understanding that we will never make it on our own. Here is the personal story of someone meeting the Bible for the first time and beginning to make it their own.

Helen: *"So....I became a Christian and was then presented with a book by my friend. 'Cool, I thought… let's have a read'. My obvious assumption was to start at the beginning and read through to the end, like any normal book. I think I got half way through Exodus before completely giving up due to boredom and, to be honest, not having a clue why this was meant to be helpful to my life. So for a while I put my Bible aside, not really* *understanding why Christians harped on about it so much. Then one day it was recommended to me that I should read a gospel, so after Google searching 'gospels' I discovered Mark was the shortest of the four so I began with this. I read the whole of Mark in one night as I just loved it. I knew Jesus had died for me because he loved me and had then been raised to life again, but I had no idea he had done all this cool stuff during his life. It made me want to learn more about him and opened up many more books of the New Testament to me.*

I have learnt since that when I read my Bible I connect heart to heart with God. There is no better place to see the heart of God than in the gospels in the Bible. The gospel of Mark is a great place to start as it's simply written and clearly reveals the story of Jesus which shows the heart of God for us. It reveals so much about the life, death and resurrection of Jesus. Beginning at Genesis and reading from cover to cover was of no help to me in the beginning. I have learnt that the Bible is not like any other book. It is not a novel where we should just read it through once or even twice and then chuck it to the side. It is not like a textbook where we refer to it for the odd fact. The Bible is a practical gift from God to help us daily with everything that goes on in our lives. From my experience the more I read the Bible, the more and more I fall in love with it. I see the practical advice it gives to me to help me and to guide me and see now how this has changed me over the last 7 years. The more I read, the more I understand. Books in the Bible which never made sense to me begin to make so much more sense in context with the gospels.

I needed to start small though and to not aim to read a book a night as I once did, as I missed so many things by being over ambitious. I found reading small chunks at a time and thinking about them helped me most. It helped me to get a Youth Bible commentary which took me slowly through a book of the Bible and was invaluable in explaining confusing words and chunks that I didn't understand.

At first there were so many words and ideas which made no sense to me. I didn't have any family members who could explain to me what words like grace and atonement meant so it was all a little blurry. I found Christian mates to be the most help with this. A few of my friends had been Christians since they were little kids so had a much better understanding of the Christian jargon and were able to explain things to me. With time I also learnt to not be afraid of asking questions. I had felt pretty stupid in my youth group because I didn't really get what they were talking about a lot of the time. However I realised that my youth leaders were happy to answer my questions and in fact as a youth leader myself now I get a real buzz when young people ask questions about the Bible or God. I encourage you to ask as many questions as you need to as the people you're asking were once in the same place you are, so they will understand you.

Just to mention as well....I had some really big issues with feeling really rubbish if I didn't read my Bible every night for a while. I felt like I was a rubbish Christian and that God was ashamed of me for missing a day in my 'Bible schedule'. I completely misunderstood God and why he had given us the Bible in the first place. God doesn't sit and wait for us to mess up so he can condemn us for it. He's not like a big kid with a magnifying glass who enjoys using the sun to try to fry little helpless ants on an ant hill. Yes, God is way bigger than us and he is all powerful but he adores you and seeks to nurture you and protect you. He is proud of us every time we pick up the Bible to read his word, but only because he knows how good it is for us and he desperately wants the best for us. Enjoy your Bible....its class!"

Andy: Sarx is a fun word to say aloud and is the Greek word for flesh. As such it doesn't just refer to our skin, organs and muscles but the sum total of everything we are: our spirits, minds and bodies. So when John told us (John 1:14) that in Jesus, the 'Word became flesh', John was letting us know that Jesus was stepping into the fullness of humanity's experience. It is the miraculous transition of 'the Word' becoming flesh in our lives that is at the heart of being a Christian. I long to see the words of the Bible fleshed out by Jesus' now body – namely us. It's too easy to create private lives of devotion, where we are happy to simply read the words, rather than letting them become flesh in our imaginations, action and experience.

My guess is that you may struggle to keep up-to-date with daily devotionals. My personal pathetic excuse is that they have always been too passive for my taste. I am more likely to do something if I have to plan it slightly and make it an event. There is then intentionality about the time I am spending with God. I also think God notices the difference when we specifically set aside time to be with him rather than simply trundling through sleepy readings.

The other regular complaint that I hear from folks is that you may well diligently read your daily devotional guide every day for a month, but if after thirty days someone asked you what you had learned, it would all be a bit of a mush. Each day fails to stand out from the others. Now, I know that it is not all about memory and that the daily 'washing of the word' is a spiritual discipline that has a positive effect on our lives, whether it reaches a conscious mental level or not, but why leave it at that? Time after time, as we have experimented with experiential learning, you find that people remember passages and concepts because they can say, oh yes – that was the day when we lit a fire, or got to the top of the car park. Not only does this build up a library of firm memories but it creates a real-world faith that means we have spiritual associations popping into our heads the next time we are involved in the activity that was part of the devotion (e.g. doing the dishes or walking in the park).

Like me, you probably don't like people telling you to do things. I don't mind people suggesting that I read things, because then I retain some control. But telling me what to *do*? It makes me feel like I'm back in my youth group again! You know, that might not necessarily be a bad thing. If you're anything like me, back then, you probably had a healthier attitude to learning and letting that learning influence your lifestyle. As adults we like to think that we have it sorted and that any obvious attempt at discipline would be an admission of failure for our way of doing things (perish the thought!) The moments when I have noticed change effected in my own life are those moments when I have allowed God to speak to me through his Word while I have processed, meditated and ruminated on it through some form of activity.

A cautionary note – this is definitely not about replacing stillness in God's presence for manic activity – I've been trying that all my life, and it doesn't work! It's about making full use of all the resources God has given us for interacting and learning about him. After all, the disciples weren't exactly bookish. We often forget that for most of Church history not many people had their own Bible. Only in the last 100 years or so has that even become a possibility! Somehow everyone still lived Christian lives before then, experiencing God through community reading and action. Is Bible reading just one more thing that we have privatised and commoditized?

Don't get me wrong. I love reading Bible stories and the great illustrative stories that devotional writers tell as much as the next person. They have informed many of my opinions and attitudes. But I want more. I don't want to just read the story. I want to be part of the story – God's big story. Books like God360 provide you with many 'access points' where you can step into the story. You see the story of God is organic and evolving. It changes because you've started to play your part.

Suggestions you'll read in the Bible from other folks who have been running this marathon are simply snippets of advice from the "Lonely Planet guide to following Jesus". These people have travelled ahead of us, and done some scoping out, so that we don't make their mistakes, and so we enjoy the best views on the journey. This is not a book of regulations which, if fulfilled, will make God like you. That's not what the Bible is about. That's why Jesus said, 'My yoke is easy, and my burden is light.' (Matthew 11:30). He already does love us. He was continually berating the Pharisees for piling even more regulations onto people. The Big Story of the Bible is that he loves us so much; he is inviting us to be part of seeing his broken world put to rights. Of seeing people made whole, of seeing people have enough, of seeing people free from addictions, of seeing people come together, of seeing compassion, mercy, forgiveness and purity exploding from the pores of humanity. God wouldn't call us to this life of sacrifice if he hadn't gone there himself, and if he didn't know it was the way we were designed to live, before our hot-headed independence kicked in.

Following Jesus isn't the easiest life possible, but I honestly believe it's the best life possible. It's an adventure where you are stretched to put the needs of others before yourself, and therefore to be part of transforming the world. For years, folks have wrongly seen "becoming a Christian" as simply an escape ticket for heaven, when it's also about bringing heaven to earth. In every thought and action we can be part of people being released from the stuff that holds them back in life, to be more fully who they were created to be.

DRINK STATION THREE:

The People You Run With

Andy: *"The day has arrived and the crowd throngs before the starting tape. Last minute tension sings through your taut nerves. You are wondering whether you have it in you to reach the finish, the others beside you look more experienced, fitter, somehow better equipped when the gun goes off and together you move as one onto the slick grass, funnelling down until there can be only one leader. It is not you. You cannot even see them because of the mass of bodies you now find yourself running alongside. You start your watch as you shuffle across the line and watch for some space in which to find your stride. But until then you are comforted that you are neither first, nor last, or by yourself. You are in the race and running and it feels good."*

Feeling good is a good feeling, but when you are running it is tinged with the knowledge that it won't last. Paul wrote in Acts 20:24 that he considered the race he was running to be more valuable than even his own life, so desperate was he to share the goodness of God's amazing grace. What would be worth your while giving your all for like the boy who finds treasure in a field and in his joy sells everything he has just to purchase the field and hold onto the treasure? (Matthew 13:44)

33

Daley Thompson was a decathlete in the 1980's who was famous for training even on Christmas day so that when he lined up to start a race he knew he had given his all to the cause. This kind of commitment can be really hard to accept if you figure on going it alone, but the good news is that the marathon of faith is not a solo race. It's a team sport. God is a team (made up of the Father, the Son (Jesus) and the Holy Spirit), and because we're made to be like God, we are designed to need each other. It's really hard to admit to needing anyone in our lives, and in fact much of our communication revolves around trying to prove that "we're fine, thanks very much". We think that to admit our need would be to admit weakness, and leave us vulnerable to others taking advantage of us. We try to project an image of being strong, when inside we're all broken people. This all comes back to whether we see life as a team sport or as a competition. If it's a competition, then of course we'll pretend to be strong, in case we give any of our competitors an advantage. And we won't stop to help anyone else because that would slow us down.

Everything around us screams that life is a competitive race. People are competing for fame, and for attention on our TV screens, and all of us have had the experience of competing for our parents' love with brothers and sisters or the other demands on their time. So it's not surprising that we falsely believe that we need to compete for God's love. Jesus tells a story (Luke 19) about a dysfunctional family traditionally called 'The Prodigal Son'. A father has two sons and the younger son rudely asks for his inheritance while his father is still alive. He then wastes all the cash living a Premiership footballer lifestyle before returning home in fear, penniless and hoping to be re-employed. Instead of receiving an ear-bashing he has a party thrown in his honour, as his father is so glad to have him home. His older brother has never left home and diligently served his father all this time. In a fit of jealousy he screams at his father that he has never had a party thrown for him, even though he has been a model son. We know what he means. We identify with his sense of injustice. But the reason we do is that we too have bought into the lie that life is a competition. We subliminally compete with each other for God's love and approval, believing that our efforts will be rewarded with his love. The father in the story responds by making it clear that if that was what his son was trying to do, he was wasting his time, because his son already had all he owned. He says, "All I have is yours." (Luke 15:31). Competing with fellow humans makes no sense in the face of unconditional love. It is endless. There is not a finite amount that has to be divided up amongst us, just like fame or money, thereby causing the inevitable competition. There is enough to go round, yet we still act as if more for her means less for me. We're in this together.

As the African proverb says, "If you want to go quickly, go alone, but if you want to go far, go together."

We are now so used to being consumers with our remote controls and a million choices; we can easily see church as just another lifestyle choice. It's not a place where we'll simply go to consume whatever is thrown at us. It's a community where we will also be able to give. We will be able to contribute.

Mark: Can I be a Christian and not go to church? You can, but it's a bit like a footballer playing football down in the park on his own. Ultimately, you'll give up, and it won't be much fun. Christianity is designed as a team sport. In fact God himself is a team. He exists as Father, Son and Holy Spirit all working together in committed relationships of love. And because we are made in his image, we operate as we're meant to, when we are in meaningful committed relationships. The truth is that to ask the question, "Do I need to go to church to be a Christian?" is perhaps asking the wrong question. The fact that we ask it betrays the fact that we think about everything these days from an individual point of view. So we're left thinking, what's the least I need to commit to get away with being sorted with God? We've missed the point. If we truly love God, we will love others and desire to give our lives to them. God wants the best for us, and he knows we become our true selves when we interact with others. This interaction improves us, as it rubs off our hard edges, and forces us to be less selfish.

So get involved with a group of people that are engaged with their community and praying for God to move supernaturally in that community. In our personal lives we need a healthy balance between intimacy and involvement, and this is true for our churches as well. With a focus on intimacy only, we are left with our head in the clouds, but are of no earthly good to anyone. With a focus only on involvement, we quickly run out of fuel for the journey, as we engage with the reality of a broken world. When we are exercising both disciplines, we start to realise that they aren't in fact separate. We truly get to know God as we serve, and the closer we draw to him, the more he downloads his heart to us, and draws us to those in need.

Here's a personal view from someone who's running alongside you.

Helen: *"Before becoming a Christian I had a very negative view of church. I thought it was boring, irrelevant and full of old biddies that were way too over enthusiastic about tea and biscuits. I would have rather repeatedly jammed my tongue in a door than attend church to be perfectly honest so was well aware that finding a new church was going to be a challenge. My friend went to what he described as a* *'lively charismatic church' which meant very little to me at the time. I agreed to go along one week with a friend who had also just become a Christian.*

It was a shock to the system to say the least. To put it in to context I had hung around until this point with a group of mates who liked to get high on drugs at weekends. To walk into a church and see people similarly excited and enthusiastic meant that my natural question to my friend was, 'Why are these people all high?' It took patience and understanding on his behalf to explain that in fact they weren't high on drugs, just enthusiastic and passionate about God. Nevertheless having only been to a church where enthusiasm was directed towards cups of tea, the following weeks were a major adjustment period for me, largely spent naming the extraordinary people who attended this church. There was 'picnic lady' who liked to rustle tin foil as she got her sandwiches out ready for the sermon; 'cub scout man' (because he reminded us of an over-enthusiastic scout leader) who led worship; and keemanaanbread lady who appeared to recite Indian takeaway menus whilst praying in some strange language (which I later understood to be a biblical language called tongues).

So, as you can see, I was a highly confused and somewhat bewildered 13 year old when I first went to this 'happy-clappy' church (which is what I quickly translated lively charismatic to mean at the time). I'm not going to pretend that in a mere few weeks I adjusted to this new environment; in fact it took months! What I will say, however, is that I am so pleased I stuck with it. Sometimes it was only my mates in my youth group which kept me going but just having Christian friends around me was of enormous benefit to me. Over time and almost subconsciously regular teaching in church and youth meetings and support from friends and youth leaders helped me understand and get to grips with church and its peculiarities.

Seven years later and church still has its fair share of funny people...indeed 'cub scout man' and 'picnic lady' still exist but I see church more like a family now. We all have quirky relatives with peculiar characteristics and church is no different. But you know this is one of the things which is so great about church. Look at Jesus...He was a homeless bloke who did very peculiar things like raise the dead, or look at John who ate locusts and wild honey! Yet Jesus is the head of the Church and John was a key figure in the early church. Church is open to everyone, including me and you, no matter what our quirks may be. Although church was tough for me at first it has been so important in my personal journey with God.

To find a church: pray about it; see where friends and family go and try churches out; decide on one; and then get stuck in to it. I went to my church because my mate went there and this was a great support to me. I go now because I love church, I love the people, I love to hear teaching about Jesus and I love to worship God with other Christians."

Andy: At the end of the day, the church is made up of flawed human beings. Much as we'd rather be members of clubs and societies where everyone is perfect, (like us!), this is sadly not the case. Once we're part of the family we discover that forgiveness is like breathing out, impossible unless you are also breathing in. In this case the breathing in is being made more like Jesus by the Holy Spirit knocking off our rough edges. Shakespeare wrote in Hamlet that, 'There is a divinity that shapes our ends, rough hew them though we will,' and that is what the Holy Spirit does.

If we do not let the Holy Spirit shape us then we will always remain cynical of church and miss the wood for the trees, or the speck for our plank (Luke 6:41-42). Church is glorious because of its flaws. Why? Because those flaws include each of us, rough hewn though we are.

Church is set up for the sharing of God's grace to those he created and loved, i.e. everyone. Sometimes it forgets that it is a lifesaving operation, but only when we forget that first. The church is, after all, the people and not the building and so wherever followers of Jesus are gathered together, church is. This is for our sustaining and maturing as Christians, but primarily it is to bring the truth that sets us free (John 8:31) to bear in the world we live in – e.g. by providing food and shelter for those in need, because we recognise that we are loved unconditionally by God and so loving others becomes more of a reflex action, or by spending time campaigning for injustices in our country and abroad to end because we take more time to care about what God cares about and then act accordingly. Maybe we can pick a country that has gone unnoticed or forgotten, like Gabon or Dominica, and learn about it and pray about it, even sponsor a child who lives there to help us remember that we are all God's children. Perhaps we can share the truth of Jesus in our words and deeds in our place of work, around the family mealtime, at the gym or by the school gates: whatever you choose they each make earth a lot more like heaven, one day at a time, one issue at a time and one person at a time. Not on our own, not only together, but together with God. We sometimes procrastinate, waiting for the right thing, when there is all this need constantly around us. Jim Wallis, the American activist, says this, "Find a great need in the world, and find what you're good at. Where those two things intersect – that's what you should spend your life doing." Why not start now?

Perhaps you don't know where to start. Well, look at where you live, where you work and any other locales you frequent by going to the gym or school or visiting family. Type that place name into an internet search engine (free internet access is available at every local library) and then add the word church. See what comes up and email the contact to arrange a free cup of tea, complimentary biscuit and a gratis visit. Don't believe it works? Well, my wife and I have just chosen where to move to next on the strength of the local church using this exact method. (Except we may have been offered coffee instead of tea if my memory serves me correctly) If following Jesus is that worthwhile, why not move for church reasons instead of just for job or family reasons?

You Find Yourself Out On Your Own

Andy: *"The race is now well under way. The rolling downland of the opening few miles has been replaced by a circuit looping around a disused gravel pit. The going is treacherous and slippery, the route monotonous and the scenery depressing. An abandoned car sticks out of the discoloured water like a rusty duck, up tail and dabbling. Worse, though, is the fact that even though you can see other runners you are out on your own. You feel terribly lonely all of a sudden, and keenly need someone to know your name and ask if you are alright, perhaps even throw an arm around you. You smile for no reason and then realise that you are about to move onto the next section; the fells. Despite this hazard you keep smiling as a lead runner has appeared just in front of you having seemingly just finished repairing a badly snapped lace. He begins to chat as the fells draw closer and before you notice he is sharing the view from the top with you. With a spring in your steps you advance together towards the next peak."*

Jesus loved being by himself, not so he could wash the troublesome disciples out of his hair for a few hours, but so that he could spend some quality time praying. Have a look at Matthew 14. Jesus hears that his cousin John has just been beheaded, for staying faithful and following God despite being unpopular with powerful people. Verse 13 sees him try to withdraw to a solitary place, but the crowds follow him. He has compassion on them and heals them and then feeds them miraculously, all before he eventually leaves both the crowd and his disciples to climb a mountain and pray (v.23). Jesus aches to spend time with his Father in prayer, but loves those around him before he indulges in that quality time he so desires. Have you ever felt that dependant upon anything? Do you think prayer could ever become that important to you?

People sometimes think that prayer is a mystical and formal religious set-piece. It can be turned into that, but mostly it is a relationship: making room to chat with God.

Why not start now? Jamie Oliver is on a mission to get us all cooking, but the only way to really pick it up is by watching others do it, whether in our kitchens or on the TV. So in that spirit of picking stuff up from others, here's a prayer that I sometimes pray.

"Lord, I think you're amazing. I don't totally understand why you love me or want to interact with me, but you do, and I'm so grateful for that. Help me today to be everything you've made me to be. Amen"

We can speak to God through prayer, and because he is our friend and helper, we can talk to him naturally and easily. We don't have to use a special voice or special words. He is a friend that loves you and is listening.

Part of the point of prayer is not so much what we say, but how it orientates us. It gives us a chance of living lives that are orientated towards God, because we are regularly acknowledging that he is the source of life, love and everything else we enjoy in creation. Starting the day with an attitude of gratitude makes such a difference to our mood. We live in a society where we expect and even demand certain rights, so when we don't get something or even if something is delayed, we get angry and feel we're not getting what we're due. We have started to regard life as a right rather than a gift. If we start a day giving thanks for life and what the day will bring, there is a much better chance that we will be thankful for it as we go through it, and that we can enjoy it with open hands that could bless others along the way, rather than simply grabbing what we feel we're owed.

This came home to me very strongly when a group from our church visited a school for orphaned girls in Uganda. These girls have been brought up by strangers or distant family members and live in pretty horrendous conditions in the slums. Yet every morning when we pulled in through the gates of the school, we could hear the sound of singing. There were about one hundred voices raised, alongside much clapping and dancing. It was a joyous sight.

These girls, who in the world's eyes had absolutely nothing, were celebrating and giving God praise, purely because he was God. When I wait until later in the day to connect with God, I am inevitably bringing him a shopping list because I am already into the busyness of everything I want to do. There is something incredibly powerful about letting God be God, not Santa! I fear many of our attitudes to prayer spring from childhood communications with Santa! In the words of my beautiful niece, "You tell Santa what you want and then you get it"

So who are we praying to? A head teacher or cheerleader? How you imagine God has a massive impact on what you say to him. We subtly shift our vocabulary and our honesty depending on whom we are speaking to. You can see this everyday of our lives, in the different ways you talk to your work colleagues, your children, or your spouse.

Where do you most enjoy hanging out and chatting? If it's in your local coffee shop, then imagine sitting in a soft seat and chatting to God there. If it's sitting on a barstool in your local pub then imagine chatting to God there. If it's walking in the countryside, then imagine chatting to God there. And sometimes you won't need to be doing any talking – you'll just be listening, or maybe you'll just be sitting in silence enjoying each other's presence and resting from the madness of life.

Mark: Recently I spent two hours on the train to London and I couldn't believe how tired everyone looked. And this was a Monday morning, when everyone is meant to be refreshed from the weekend. I wondered how this same trainload of people was going to look by Friday afternoon.

Whether we admit it or not, we all desperately need to know that someone is on our side. Many of the folks on that train looked as if they were doing life solo, and you could see it in their faces. I wondered when was the last time that they heard someone say, "Well done. Keep going. I really appreciate you."

As you will have gathered, I love stories – so let me tell you another. A friend of mine, Neil, was hiking with others in the Lake District. At one point they were walking along a road when, all of a sudden, a car came screeching up beside them.

Inside the car was a father who told them about how his son was on a mission to cycle from John O'Groats to Lands End. The dad explained how his son wasn't far away on the road, but the problem was he was struggling and had been talking of giving up. The man asked if they would mind helping him cheer on the young man as he passed by in the next couple of minutes. They, along with a few other hikers, agreed. Some inexperienced cheer leaders had been recruited!

Shortly afterwards, the son came cycling round the corner. He looked shattered because the hills had taken it out of his young legs. The small crowd began to cheer, with the cyclist's father giving the loudest and most passionate encouragements. As the son heard the cheers, it gave him strength and he pushed and sped on towards the finish. When the cyclist had become a spec in the distance, his father shook the hands of those who had stopped and thanked them. He explained that he was going to gather another crowd further ahead in order to help his son remain encouraged.

This is how it is for us on this journey of Christianity. There are times when it is hard and we feel like giving up. Yet God is our greatest supporter. He thinks we are amazing and is with us every step of the way. He will continue to surprise us by bringing people into our lives to encourage, if we let them in. This is the church.

Church: a family of forgiven sinners. Now, sin is a word that often scares people. Too often we think of sin as a list of "thou shalt not's", like puddles on a footpath which we have to tiptoe through, trying to avoid them. This way of thinking leaves us wanting to pull on the wellies that we wore as a five year old and just tramp through those puddles to have some rebellious fun. The origins of the word sin lie in the image of an archer failing to hit her target. You may want to imagine the multi-coloured concentric circles that Olympic archers aim at. The word describes the arrow not even making it as far as the target, but falling short way before it. This is sin. We will simply never love perfectly as God loves. We fall way short. That is our lot as humans and we're stuck with it. Whether our arrows limp to a few metres from our feet or just graze the target doesn't matter. We won't make it. So why do we compete with our fellow humans when we're all in the same boat? We do it to make us feel alright because "at least we're better than they are." Christianity is not about being better than anyone. It's actually about accepting that we're all a bit messed up, and that we all make many decisions every day that hurt or ignore those around us. The good news is that if we choose to accept the embrace of God, we discover that his forgiveness is total, and has been waiting there all along. In the face of this love, we lay down our independence, and confess that we aren't perfect. But we do this in response to this love, rather than as a prerequisite for being loved.

Church is the place where we experience and express forgiveness in prayer with other forgiven sinners. We can return to God here, even when we know we have done wrong, like the prodigal son (Luke 15). It is here that we can discover with others how our expectations of ourselves and of God can be way wide of the mark and pick up, and indeed be picked up by, those around us; rather than give up at the first sign of tiredness or spiritual cramp. Church is where we best see what it means to be adopted in the family of God; where we can learn more about our loving, forgiving father. Prayer is the first step we take for ourselves on that journey.

Many have been running this race for centuries and have found these ancient ways of keeping on track. Why don't we make good use of their wisdom? If they needed discipline to avoid distractions in the sixteenth century, how much more do we need simple disciplines today? Have a look at the books by Francis De Sales, Julian of Norwich, Thomas à Kempis and Ignatius of Loyola for a flavour of these self same simple disciplines.

Mark: I was on this coast-to-coast bike ride, and hit a horrendous hill. I was really struggling, but then remembered I had PowerAde in my backpack, and I sucked what seemed like litres into my dry mouth. It surprised me how much it re-energised me, so I was able to get to the top of the hill. We like to think that we are self-sufficient – that we have everything within us that we will need for life's journey. But the reality is that we all need inspiration and fuel from outside of ourselves, and Jesus spoke to his followers about this process. "I will send you another comforter." (John 15:26)

Jesus' disciples were transformed from scared individuals hiding in a locked room to a confident team that would change the course of history by the filling of his Spirit. Still today Christians become channels for God to do extraordinary things, when they allow themselves to be filled with him. This might be seeing someone healed from a disease, or bringing release to someone from lies that they have believed about themselves, or running a soup kitchen for the homeless.

The Holy Spirit is not an impersonal force, but a person. In fact, this is God in us, enabling us to overcome our own limitations and selfishness to serve and impact our world.

Here is another personal story of a fellow runner in the marathon on what started to happen when they prayed.

Helen: *"It pretty much felt like I was talking to myself at first. I had assumed that prayer would be exactly like a conversation with anyone else: I would say something and God would say something back. How he would do this...I had no idea....but I expected it. It seemed rather rude of Him when he didn't reply.*

After a few weeks of frustrated rants at God for not answering, I decided to just let Him do the talking and I was going to just sit there and give him the floor. From there I realised that in order for God to speak to me I had to actually give him some time to talk. I learnt to pray by not just talking but also listening, by just sitting there thinking about God but not say anything. It was great, as having given him some time, God actually began to talk to me and answer my prayers in practical ways. I remember praying for one of my friends at school to become a Christian and 3 months later they were coming to my youth group and another 2 months after that they became a Christian. I learnt that God answers prayers but in his own perfect timing. I learnt that sticking with prayer about something or somebody actually worked.

As my relationship with God developed I began to understand that answers to my prayers came from different places and in varying time frames. I think that God uses the Bible to answer many of our prayers, as well as the people around us. I'm a very visual person and God often uses pictures to talk to me about things and answer prayers. It's not all fluffy and white though. Sometimes the answers aren't what you want to hear and can be quite challenging. When I became a Christian it was at a youth event called ninth hour. At the time I was really on a low. I used to hang out at my best friend's house at weekends where we would spend time with her brother and his mates who were 5/6 years older than us. They used to pop class A drugs and drink heavily as if it were sweets and water. I had started to try to fit in by taking some of the less hard core drugs and swigging vodka at weekends. The guys used to get really aggressive and full on when they had been popping Es and I used to be petrified of them, but obviously act cool. They would try to take advantage when they were doped up and the whole situation just felt awful. I felt so small and so worthless.

A friend invited me to go to this Christian event and after much persuasion I agreed to go. After hearing an amazing preach about Jesus and his love for me I simply said to God 'If you exist show me'. He gave me a vivid picture of a whirlpool and me being sucked in to it. Then a huge hand reached down in to it and picked me up and pulled me out and wrapped an arm around me. It made no sense to me, of course, but I knew it was God. I became a Christian that evening. A couple of months later though, when I had worked out the whole prayer business a bit more, God challenged me to stop hanging around with those guys. I didn't want to hear this as I had a sort of cool respect off some of my mates for hanging out with older people but I knew I had to stop. It was hard but God knew what was best for me.

Praying can definitely be difficult at first but it takes courage to just step out and talk to God. My whole approach to prayer has gradually changed to being more about faith: having faith that God will answer me and having faith that even when it's not what I want to hear that answer is the best thing for me."

What is it that you would most like to say to God? If saying it aloud is too scary, why not scribble it on the blank space below?

DRINK STATION FIVE:

You Have Someone to Run Beside You

Andy: *"With your eyes straining on the mountains ahead, you realise the fells behind you were nothing but good training for what is to come. Your companion has settled into a rhythm alongside you and together you lift your eyes up to scout for the path through the tree line. The route runs steeply up a narrow gully, but you spot a slightly wider more appealing pine needle path outside the marked route. Your companion tells you he has run this race before and knows that the easy appearance is deceptive and he'll keep running up the gully. You pause for a moment as he falls silent, only your breathing can be heard: then a deafening crash as a branch falls from an old fir tree, straight onto the pine needle path. Again silence and then the sound of breathing, but this time yours is twice the rate and half the depth of your calm companion. You proceed up the steep gully when, from its lip, you spy the next drink station a few miles down the lee slope. Your pace quickens and with breathless thanks to your companion for his advice, you descend towards refreshment."*

Where does your help come from? Those moments you need advice, a strong set of shoulders, hard cash no questions asked, to whom do you turn? Psalm 121 tells us that Jesus is right beside us, always. Sometimes we decide to look for the cavalry to come to our aid from distant hillsides like in a Sunday afternoon western when that will never happen. This is doubly foolish when we come to realise that the creator of the universe is by our side. Sometimes we know this presence and enjoy it; sometimes it is known but unwanted. The worse case is though when it is unknown, but needed. Turn to Jesus and receive a welcome like the little children in Mark 10:16. Where does our help come from?

Is it Jesus?

Helen: *"My opinion of Jesus was that he was some bloke who liked to tell everyone what to do and how they were doing it wrong. So when I first became a Christian I wasn't sure what his crack was. I had always thought Jesus was fictional but if He did exist He was pretty boring and condemning anyway so not the type of bloke I wanted to know. It was when I heard a preacher talking about Jesus in a completely different way that I started to wonder. I remember being told that Jesus loved me so much that He went to a cross to die for me so I could know Him. He loved me enough to go through pain and suffering just so He could call me His child. This was so different to the Jesus I had heard described by some other people. This Jesus I wanted to know. I remember also being told that being a Christian did not mean you had a boring dull life but actually an exciting adventurous life.*

Looking back, I have seen again and again God's love for me over the past years. I have seen him carry me through good times and bad times; support me despite my rebellion and just love me unconditionally just how I am. My life has been so much more exciting since I became a Christian. I have done things which I would never have done otherwise. When I was 16 years old God gave me a burning heart for going to Africa. When I was 17 years old I went to Africa for 5 weeks and had the most amazing time. I prayed for months about this that God would make my parents be happy for me to go and that he would provide for me financially as I was still at school. In three months God provided me with all the £1500 I needed to go and the approval from my parents. Jesus can do amazing things. He is totally 100% the best thing that ever happened to me. I love Him more and more each day as I get to know Him better and better. He's my best friend and He's worthy of giving your life to in order to get to know Him better and go on amazing exciting adventures with Him."

Andy: The other reason not to lapse into intense navel-gazing is that following Jesus is not just another form of self-help. There are hundreds of books available that will tell you how to improve your life. In our consumer-orientated society, this could be just another thing to consume to add to your life. We desperately grab for the cool new gadget, the up and coming artist, or the shiny new product in an attempt to improve our lives. This is not that. Jesus said, "Whoever finds his life will lose it, and whoever loses his life for my sake will find it." (Matt 10:39). Following Jesus is basically what it says on the tin – following Jesus. Simple as that. Getting a sense of how the only perfect human ever lived and making a stab at following his way of life. Back in the marathon, it's like tucking into the slipstream of the guy running in front of us. Gloriously, it takes the pressure off us. He's thinking about the route and the pace we're running at, so that we don't have to. He's taking the wind in his face so that we don't have to. We will be led into all manner of adventure and life rhythms, but it will spring from a desire to develop a meaningful relationship with him, not for reasons of religion, or trying to impress others.

We've become so used to conditional love that we don't believe that someone could love us with no strings attached. We are conditioned by society that love will only be forthcoming once we have earned it. Unconditional love is so alien today that we can actually fear it as something freakish. The unspoken mantras are "I'll love you for as long as I find you attractive", "I'll love you for as long as you entertain me", or "I'll love for as long as is socially advantageous". So when someone comes along saying "I love you. Full stop", it takes more than a little bit of processing.

We are left believing that relationships can only form when we have first proved ourselves in some way. The pattern we follow in church services often hasn't helped this. We start by confessing our sins, become cleansed of them and then are able to approach God, often through the set-piece of communion or the Eucharist. To the casual observer or participant, it can reinforce the view that we are only able to communicate with God once we have gone through a certain process, or done certain things to impress him, to gain his love. This couldn't be further from the truth. The more accurate way (and the more freeing way) to see things is this.

God loves us. Full stop. He can't not love us. It is his very nature to love us no matter how much we have ignored him. In the way that love tends to do, this changes us. In response to this love we may spend time with the God we love. We may pray to him and read about him. We may even sing to him. We may follow him by serving his people and giving sacrificially of our time and resources. But we do these things **in response** to his love, NOT in an attempt to win it. If we'd allow ourselves to believe that, this offers us a life of freedom where an impossible weight is lifted from our shoulders.

This all reminds me of a story of someone else who was on a journey. They weren't, however, permitted to get directly to their destination as they were mugged. You may have heard the story of the Good Samaritan (Luke 10:25-37). We often think that it is a story merely taking the time to stop and care for those who are struggling. But Jesus told the story in response to someone who asked him, "What must I do to inherit eternal life?" As he often did, Jesus got the man to answer his own question, "Love the Lord your God with all your heart and soul and mind, and love your neighbour as yourself." This beautiful simplicity wasn't enough for the inquisitor, however, so he asked, "But who is my neighbour?" This led to the telling of the story, illustrating that this Samaritan enemy was actually a neighbour. Jesus was telling him that to inherit eternal life you simply needed to love God and love your neighbour. But hang on, if he was saying that to love your neighbour was to love absolutely everyone you come across, from whatever race, tribe or tongue, that's a bit of a challenge. You have to selflessly love every shopkeeper, hairdresser, beggar and businessman you interact with on a daily basis, not to mention our global neighbours who we affect with our mass consumption. That's beginning to sound impossible! I certainly can't do that. I don't have that much love in me, even if I had the presence of mind to even remember to. As humans, it is impossible to love perfectly. I think I might just give up. And that is exactly where Jesus wants us to get to. He wants us to realise that we will never love perfectly. We will never get even close to how he perfectly loves us, so how could we possibly believe that we can win his favour or love by being good at life? We don't even get close! He wants us to realise that only through accepting this free gift of grace and love can we know him. In this relationship, his love is not based on anything we do to impress him. He simply loves us as his children.

DRINK STATION SIX:

The Finish Line

Andy: *"With innumerate drink stations passed and with your companion faithfully maintaining contact with you even when you faltered, the finish line approaches surprisingly quickly. As you draw ever closer to its abrupt tape and signage you chat with your companion about all that you have seen and overcome together. You wonder aloud what your friends have thought of your efforts and reflect that they were not very visible or vocal supporters. But the warmth of kinship that you feel together as you lope along eclipses the fleeting scorn of acquaintance. Again you smile as the sun shines with a warmth worthy of its final dawn on an eternal day. In peace, together, you finish the race."*

With Joe Calzaghe retiring as undefeated champion in over 40 boxing fights, the cliché, 'he fought a good fight,' was never needed. But when Paul wrote that same phrase almost two thousand years ago, it was because his race was almost over. (2 Timothy 4:7). He had kept the faith and endured to the end of the marathon. He had finished. Have you started?

So come on, continue this race that will take the rest of your life. Rosie Ruiz famously won the Boston marathon of 1980. No-one could believe how fresh he was as he raced away to the finish line. What folks didn't realise until some minutes later was that he had only run the last mile of the race! He had sneaked onto the course in a quiet spot and sped away from the other competitors. In a world of instant everything, we want everything sorted now, but there are no short cuts.

So take hold of the sponge or grab the cup of water that is being held out to you. Running this life with Jesus as both your running mate, screaming supporter and your final goal, is not the easiest life possible, but it's definitely the best life possible. You can sit and watch the race or you can get in it. That's where you'll need to breathe deeply, but you'll feel alive.

One of people's biggest fears about Christianity is often, "But what will I have to change?" The reality is that we are all in a constant process of change every day, as we are impacted by different people and situations around us. The more important question is "are we changing for the better or for the worse?" The good news is that Christianity is about a relationship of love with Jesus. Any of you who have been in love know that something changes internally that causes you to act differently. Suddenly you are happy to give up your Saturdays to do things that you never previously wanted to do. Suddenly your hard opinions on various subjects have softened slightly.

As our relationship with Jesus develops, we will change for the better. I, for one, am very glad of this fact. I know that if I was left to my own devices I would stay pretty selfish. Following Jesus will lead us to the people and places that he most cares about, who others might ignore. They may be folks that we've previously avoided, because they are annoying to spend time with, or because they simply aren't cool.

You may be reading this and thinking, "Hang on, this all sounds like more than religion. This sounds like it would take over my whole life!" Mmmmm, in a word – yes. That's the whole point. This is a change in perspective that is totally freeing. It's about a total change in your reason for running the race. It's about living your life for the sake of others and to give credit to God, rather than to gain status for yourself. It's a release from doing things, wearing things or saying things in an attempt to be loved, because you already know you are. It's a release from a state of chronic attention-grabbing behaviour because we already know we have someone's attention 24/7! Are you not feeling more relaxed already? This is the moment to pull off a mask and costume and say, here I am, warts and all, in the sure-fire knowledge that you won't be rejected. It is deeper and wider than just putting in an appearance at your local church building once a week like some sort of glorified social club. Who wants to do that anyway?

This is about discovering meaning and purpose for your whole life. This is about discovering someone who won't just be a useful little addition to your life – an interesting talking point at lunch in the office, a reason to take the kids to Sunday school, or a way to feel slightly less guilty at a Christmas carol service. This is about discovering someone who will be our best friend, our guide, our guru, reason for living, and ultimately our Lord. I make no apology for getting that word in at the start. None of us really like authority that much, unless we agree with it. I so often hear, "Oh, I don't have a problem with authority", but when questioned that simply means, "I don't have a problem with authority if I agree with the authority." What a surprise! In our post-modern culture, where all truth is relative, we are innately suspicious of anyone saying, "this is the way". The gorgeous thing is that Jesus didn't stand up and say, "This is the way". He stood up and said, "I am the way". For anyone to say that, he was either mentally ill with a huge Messianic complex, or he was who said he was. He can't have been anything in between.

That's why admiring Jesus from a distance as simply "a decent bloke with some good ideas" makes less sense than believing that he was a dangerous madman. Please take your pick, but whatever you do, don't sit on the fence.

Throughout my life I've bumped into two different groups of people who seem to be living "life to the full". There are those who grab everything the world has to offer. They acquire the best gadgets, go on the best holidays and party like there's no tomorrow. I'm not going to pretend that these folks aren't enjoying themselves. They really are! Then there are another group who I've seen give God all of their lives; praying, loving, serving and giving to people until it hurt. They are on a mission to see people made whole and they have meaningful and purposeful lives. But I'll also tell you about the group of folks who I've noticed are most miserable. They're folks who have stuck somewhere halfway between the two. Often it's Christians who try to have a bit of the Christian experience and a bit of the world's, to "play it safe", "not be too extreme" and "not look weird". In my experience that leads to folks going through life miserable because they're permanently feeling unfulfilled. So there are two parties going on. Accept the invite to one of them. All I'll say is that only one of those parties goes on forever.

Andy: I remember being really inspired by the two guys who were the first to fly a hot air balloon all the way around the world. It was a ridiculous adventure, on which they nearly died three or four times. I was mostly excited because they beat Richard Branson! I watched an interview with them in which they said that there were two main things that kept them going on such a dangerous journey. The first one was their relationship, and the second was the new perspective they felt they had on life from the height they were at. It struck me as I listened that that was exactly how I felt about the adventure of following Jesus. It is a crazy adventure that at times has you thinking, "Why did I decide to do this?", but those same things keep me going. My relationship with Jesus is a constant when things are tough and also a beautiful simplicity when life is downright confusing. Also my perspective on the world has totally changed. I don't just see it as a place of brokenness and despair now, but also as a place of hope. My final thought was, "This certainly isn't the easiest life possible, but it's definitely the best life possible."

When we start to see the impact of God being in charge in different areas of life (people call it God's 'kingdom coming'), we start to give ourselves to being agents of that Kingdom. We see people's relationships with their families improve, or we see people get more involved with the old people in their community, or we see studying become less of a chore and find its context in the bigger picture of serving God with our lives. We start loving people unconditionally, helping those in need and campaigning for justice. We start to tell the story of the one who is writing the new chapters in our story. All the selfish stuff that we've been into suddenly starts to look pretty pathetic and time-wasting in comparison.

That is why we pray what we do in the Lord's Prayer – Your Kingdom come, your will be done, on earth as it is in heaven. (Luke 11:2) We're asking for God's influence to seep into our world more and more.

Mark: Here's another way of thinking about it. Three words, but which is scarier to hear: YOU ARE FIRED! or I LOVE YOU? On the TV show "The Apprentice", Alan Sugar fires one of his potential apprentices every week. Christianity is "The Apprentice" in reverse.

Truly following Jesus allows him to sack the boss, not the apprentice. And the boss is us. Are you willing to get out of the boss's chair, and let him sit there? We grow up so insecure these days, so it's hard to let go of control. We've all become moderate control freaks, controlling our friends and families with our moods, silences or anger. But there is incredible freedom in simply letting go. It takes a lot of the burden off us. (1 Peter 5:7). You honestly don't know how good it feels until you try it. Let someone else be in charge. Any of you who have worked for awkward bosses know that it only works well when you can trust the person whose authority you're under. This is why Jesus goes out of his way to prove that he is trustworthy. (Mark 8:31 and 16:6 for instance)

He's not an angry dictator – every day is shared through a deepening relationship – he has our best interests at heart, eternally. He knows how to run our lives better than we do. Not a finger-pointing boss who just shouts commands, but a loving father. He is an empowering boss who wants to serve us in bidding for his kingdom to come. He wants to make us part of his story. And we can't get sacked. He will never forsake us.

With Jesus as the best boss (or Lord) as the Bible calls it, it inevitably has an impact on our relationships, what goes into our bodies, where we live, how we spend money, and which websites we visit. Rather than doing things simply for our own pleasure, we want to live in a way that pleases our loving boss. The beauty of this is that when our priority is serving him, we are living life the way it was meant to be, because he designed it. When we veer off the way he designed it, we inevitably damage ourselves and others in the process, in the same way it's easy to break a new gadget if we don't follow the instructions.

If we follow the instructions though, we can enjoy the life in all its fullness (John 10:10), which is eternity itself, starting today, if we but choose to follow Jesus. Heaven is our final destination. Heaven is God's realm where everything is perfect and subject to his wisdom and rule. It's not a geographical place as we've wrongly thought down through the years. Jesus talked a lot about "The Kingdom of Heaven" and used various images to try to describe it. Like the yeast working through the dough when we make bread, it is gradually invading the realm of earth.

At the end of time, heaven and earth will fuse creating the "new heaven and a new earth". This is the first five verses of Revelation Chapter 21 – Then I saw a new heaven and a new earth, for the first heaven and the first earth had passed away, and there was no longer any sea. I saw the Holy City, the New Jerusalem, coming down out of heaven from God, prepared as a bride beautifully dressed for her husband. And I heard a loud voice from the throne saying, "Now the dwelling of God is with men, and he will live with them. They will be his people, and God himself will be with them and be their God. He will wipe every tear from their eyes. There will be no more death or mourning or crying or pain, for the old order of things has passed away."

He who was seated on the throne said, "I am making everything new!" Then he said, "Write this down, for these words are trustworthy and true."

What an amazing picture of the future. And this is not pie in the sky! This is our future. It's hard to know exactly what this amazing fusion of heaven and earth will look like, but that's not the main point. It will be perfect and we will be made perfect. That phrase "I am making everything new!" is truly amazing. We get so used to our selfishness and frailty that it's hard to even imagine what the "best of us" looks like. And it's better than that!

So can you see how this changes our perspective on the race?

Can you see how having this amazing future might inspire us towards the finish line?

The wonderful thing is that God doesn't merely want us to sit around waiting for this to occur. He invites us to be partners with him in actually bringing it about! That's why the context of the marathon is such a good way to look at life. Where's the effort and challenge if we're just sitting waiting in a departure lounge for our flight to heaven to be called? The wonderful thing is that we are forging the eternal reality by our actions. Every moment of love and kindness that we show is woven into the fabric of all eternity. We don't just sit around and wait for it to happen. We help it happen.

Andy: As a young boy, the highlight of my weekend used to be the moment where my dad would come into the house and say, "Andrew, could you come and help me wash the car?" There was a flurry of excitement involving a yellow mac, buckets and sponges. Not only was the thought of being covered in soapy suds quite fantastic, but there was a glowing pride that my dad needed my help to wash his car. That was all fine until a few years ago when a sudden realisation pulled the carpet out from under my whole worldview! My presence almost certainly lengthened the whole process, and my sections of the car definitely weren't washed as well as my dad's! So I was left wondering, why did my dad ask for my help? Slowly, I came to the undeniable and beautiful conclusion that it was because he simply wanted me to be where he was. He wanted me to be doing what he was doing. He wanted to get to know me better in the midst of a shared task. We flit around believing that God needs our help to save the world, when a Father is very simply asking us to be getting up to what he's already up to. All over the world our Father is healing the sick, restoring the broken and releasing the oppressed. He doesn't need our help, but he asks us to wash the car with him.

It is so easy to reduce knowing God to an academic or cloistered exercise, but our knowing of Him also grows in the doing. I truly believe that if we're not engaging with him in serving the poor and the needy, then there are aspects of his character we will simply never get to know. We meet Jesus in the hands, eyes and hearts of the broken. Isaiah 58:6-7 confirms that this work is a devotional act.

> 6 Is not this the kind of fasting I have chosen:
>   to loose the chains of injustice
>   and untie the cords of the yoke,
>   to set the oppressed free
>   and break every yoke?

> 7 Is it not to share your food with the hungry
>   and to provide the poor wanderer with shelter—
>   when you see the naked, to clothe him,
>   and not to turn away from your own flesh and blood?

There is also challenge here for those who like me are so busy washing the car, that they believe their own effort to be all-important. Prayer and "supernatural" experience can be seen as merely a support, or "fuel for the journey", rather than integral to the kingdom coming in all its fullness, for as we are reminded, this battle is not just about flesh and blood, whether on a personal or a structural level. Integral mission is not just putting evangelistic words and prophetic actions together, but seeing our involvement as vital to our ever-growing relationship with God.

So in the midst of all of life's confusion, I for one am glad that someone who actually lived as a historical figure and real human being is standing and saying, "I am the way!", because I certainly wouldn't have sussed what the way was, and never will. When he said, "I am the way", he was saying, "Follow me! This relationship with me is what will bring you true freedom". He was saying, "Come change the world with me, for in serving others with me, you find yourself." He was saying, "I have walked this way and I will take the blame for the stuff you do wrong, so it doesn't hang over you". He was saying, "There is a bigger picture than what you see with your eyes". He was saying, "I love you. You matter. You are unique. You have the potential for incredible beauty and goodness. Fancy giving it a go?"